Water has no color
Look at your neighbor, Look at nature

Look at your baby sister or brother

We are all made out of
a drop of water
And without water we will all be in danger

All kinds of babies
are made of
a drop of water

The duck who lives in the water
was made of a drop of water

The flower overlooking the water
Was made of a drop of water

Wild horses are made of a drop of water

Large or small
all Creatures
are made of a drop of water

Eighty percent of earth
is covered with water

Seventy five percent
of our bodies is made of water

We drink water

We play in water

We love living near water

We swim in water

we clean ourselves with water

We sail on water

We play sports in water

But did you know that no one is better
than the other
because we are all made of
the same drop of water!

We are all made
with such a wonder
From a drop of water

Now look at a small pet,
or a big fish caught in a net

Look at a jaguar swimming in the forest before breakfast

What do you have in common
if you haven't already guessed

With Cherry blossom trees

with chicks and bunny rabbit babies

That's right, we all need water

We need to drink water
Drinking water will perk us up

Just as a wilted flowers will
perk up in water

Elephants need to drink water

Giraffes need to drink water

Some flowers live on water

But did you know
that even before we were born
we lived in water

We are all connected to our surroundings,
we are all one,
and we are all made of
a drop of water

H2O

Two parts hydrogen and one part oxygen

We are made of
2 parts Hydrogen
One part Oxygen
Which is water

water is the most vital element,
next to air, to our survival

All living things
must have water to survive,
whether they get it from a water fountain,
a rain cloud, or from lakes, rivers, or oceans

Water exists even in the air
as water vapor,
and in the ground as soil moisture

Water truly is everywhere,
still most take it for granted
So take care of the water

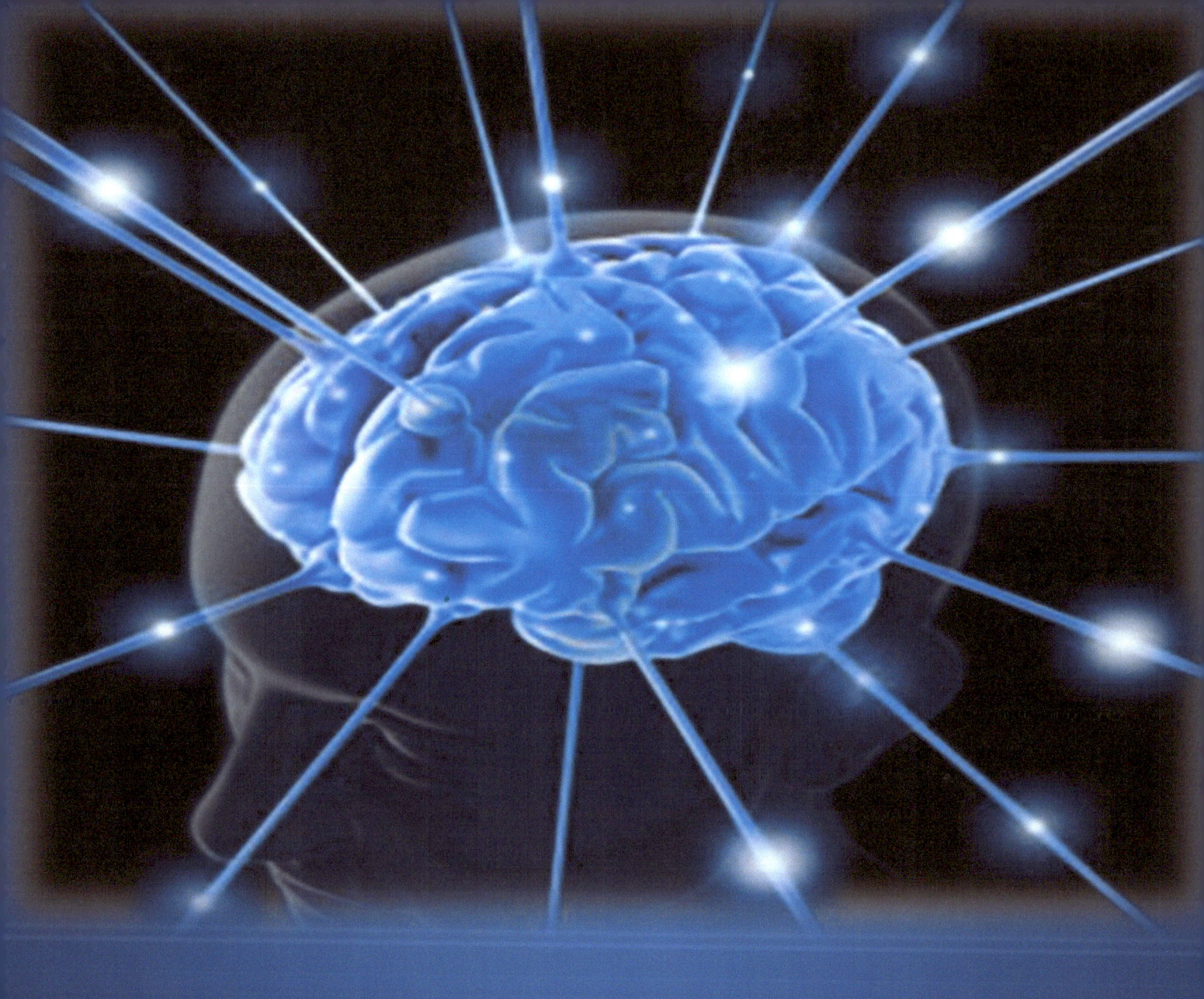

Did you know that
our brain is made mostly of water!

85%
WATER

BLOOD

And our blood is mostly made of water,
water helps digest our food,
transport waste, and control
our body temperature

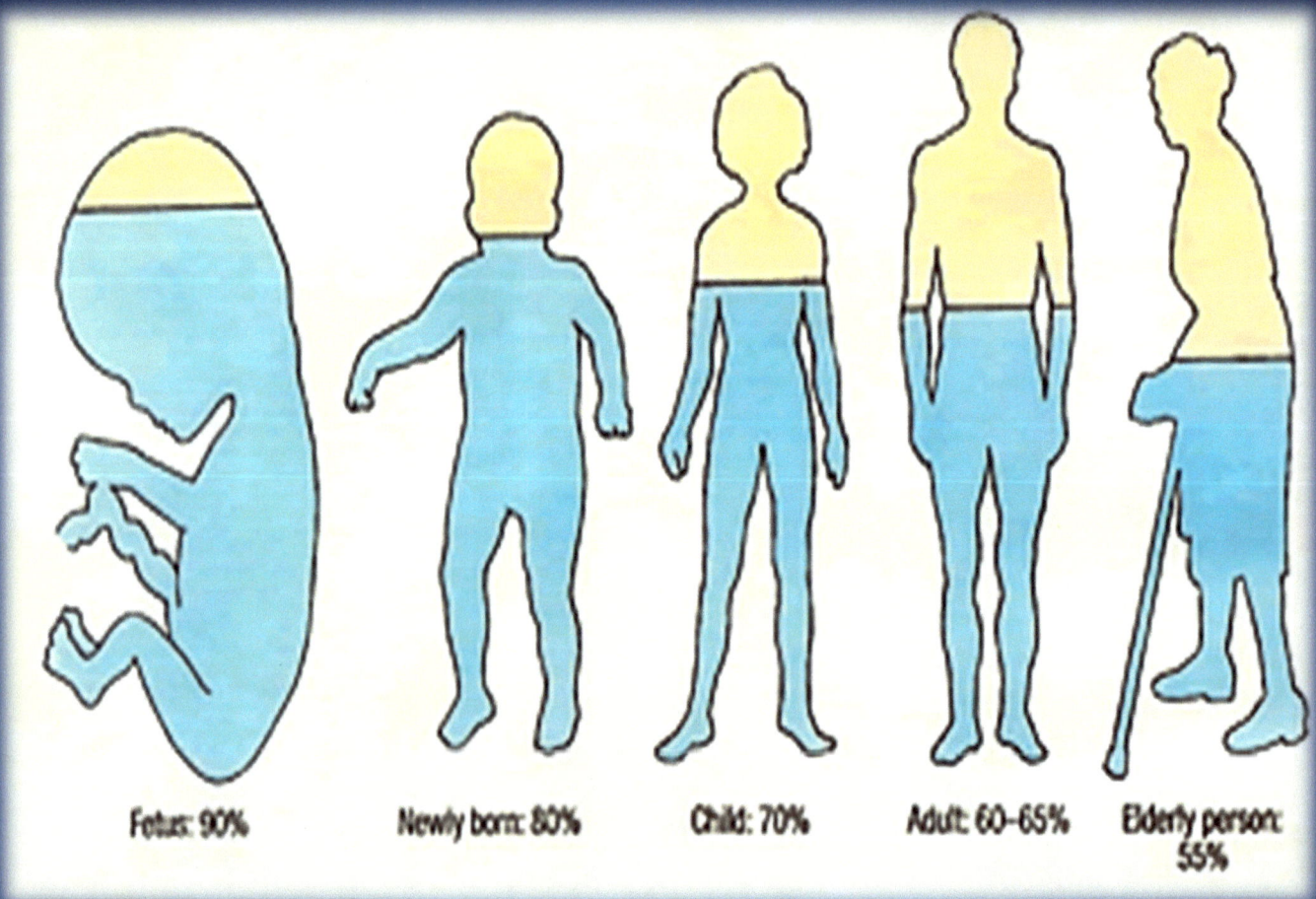

Fetus: 90%   Newly born: 80%   Child: 70%   Adult: 60-65%   Elderly person: 55%

And did you know that
babies' bodies
have more water than grownups!

Our bodies cannot work without water
just as a car cannot run without gas and oil

8

That's why we need
to drink five to eight glasses
of water each day

And any drop in our body's water
can trigger
feeling tired and worn-out
we might need to call the doctor
to make us feel better

Because all creation including
plants, stars and even rocks
are made of a drop of water

and we are all
a part of a greater One

Let us
thank our maker
for making us from a drop of water

Let us laugh and play
be happy living peacefully together

Because we are all made of a drop of Water
Make a Peace Tree
Write your acts of kindness to each other
on colored paper
and put it in the corner

Life Came From Water

The Qur'an describes that God
"made from water every living thing"
(21:30)

Another verse describes how
"God has created every living creature
from water; of them are some that creep
on their bellies, some that walk on two
legs, and some that walk on four.
God creates what He wills, for truly God
is able to do all things." (24:45)

These verses support the scientific
theory that life began in the Earth's
oceans.

www.ingramcontent.com/pod-product-compliance
Lightning Source LLC
Chambersburg PA
CBHW041517280526
45792CB00004B/1278